fruit
salad

Appliqué Designs
for Delicious Quilts

fruit salad

Appliqué Designs
for Delicious Quilts

By Bea Oglesby

Free Pattern !

See page 95
for details!

Fruit Salad

Appliqué Designs for Delicious Quilts

By Bea Oglesby

Editor: Deb Rowden

Designer: Brian Grubb

Photography: Aaron T. Leimkuehler

Illustration: Lon Eric Craven

Technical Editor: Deb McCurnin

Production assistance: Jo Ann Groves

Published by:
Kansas City Star Books
1729 Grand Blvd.
Kansas City, Missouri, USA 64108

First edition, first printing
ISBN: 978-1-933466-56-9

Library of Congress Control Number: 2008923870
Printed in the United States of America by
Walsworth Publishing Co., Marceline, MO

**To order copies, call StarInfo
at (816) 234-4636 and say "Books."**

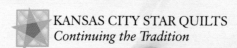

Introduction

All About Fruit

Fruit, more than any other food that we eat, is one of our most important foods. From the vine or from the tree, nothing could be sweeter. As a still life centerpiece in a bowl on a table, it provides a beautiful sight and fragrance. Fruit comes in a glorious range of color, texture, flavor, shape and size.

Most of us are familiar with fruits such as apples, pears, plums, bananas, and oranges. In days gone by, they were available only in season. Depending on where you live, many of us may have had an apple, pear, peach or perhaps a guava or mango tree in our own backyard. Many of these trees will produce a crop each year with little extra care or attention—and these trees are also a wonderful addition to our landscaping.

Nutritionists advise us to eat five servings of colorful fruits and vegetables every day. Vibrantly colored fruits are not only eye-catching, but they have an abundance of vitamins and beneficial antioxidants as well. They are also believed to protect us against a wide range of diseases including heart disease, arthritis, osteoporosis, diabetes, hypertension, and even some cancers.

With today's global economy, we are now able to enjoy most varieties of fruits year-round. This has let us become familiar with many exotic fruits from around the world. Take advantage of the fresh fruits sold at the local farmer's markets, but be adventurous and try some of the exotic fruits in the supermarket. Enjoy these fruits in a variety of ways—as a simple, perfect piece at the end of a meal, or in recipes from simple to elaborate.

Eating five servings of fruit will not be difficult— as five servings of fruit a day simply will not be enough.

How to Make These Quilts

About the Patterns

The 27 fruit patterns in this book are divided into four categories:
- Five citrus fruit: grapefruit, kumquats, lemons, limes and oranges.
- Four berries: blueberries, gooseberries, raspberries and strawberries.
- Nine exotic fruits: carambola or star fruit, fig, guava, mango, papaya, passion fruit, persimmon, pomegranate and monstera deliciosa.
- Nine common fruit: apples, cherries, grapes, kiwi, peaches, pears, pineapple, plums, and melons.

Complete patterns are provided for each fruit. You can make them as I have, in four different categories, and four different size wallhangings. You may wish to combine any or all of the fruits together into one larger quilt.

The patterns are complete on one page (which fits onto a 12" finished block) except for three: the pineapple, the grapes and the melon (these three were done on a double block). These three will fit onto a 12" block by leaving off the extra leaves of each fruit.

Each fruit can be individualized as you wish. A simple wallhanging of the single pineapple can be a welcome sign for visitors in your entrance hall. Make a tablerunner for your breakfast table with three of your favorite fruits. Simplify the patterns by leaving off the fruit cross-sections or the flower buds.

The number of pieces in the fruit patterns range from nine for the monstera deliciosa to 79 for the pineapple. The number of pineapple pieces can be reduced if one piece of fabric is used for the entire pineapple instead of cutting individual pieces. The grapes can be treated the same way, using one piece of fabric for the fruit instead of individual segments.

Appliqué techniques

I appliquéd my fruit by hand using the needle-turn method. I do this because I enjoy handwork; however, all of these patterns can be done with fusible web appliqué or machine appliqué. If you are new to quilting or to appliqué, take a basic class to learn or hone your skills, then choose the method you enjoy to create one or several of your favorite fruit blocks.

Fabric needed

Fabric amounts for the different projects are included, but other than the background fabrics and borders, scraps and fat quarters for the fruit colors are all you need. Basically, the amount of fabric needed will depend on what you plan to make. Feel free to use your own favorite colors for your fruit and background.

Tools and supplies

With appliqué, minimal equipment is needed to complete your project. Other than the background and appliqué fabrics, you need only basic sewing supplies. For this reason, I always suggest that you buy the best supplies available. Once purchased, they will last many years if properly cared for. Remember, these are a good investment and will not only make your work easier, but will also improve it.

Needles: I suggest sharps, which come in assorted sizes. Needles are numbered according to size: the higher the number, the smaller the needle. I use size 11 or 12. These needles have a narrow shank, which makes them easy to pull through the fabric and not leave holes. The use of a smaller needle results in a smaller and finer stitch.

Thread: For traditional appliqué, I use 100% cotton size 60 thread in the color that matches the appliqué piece. Silk thread is

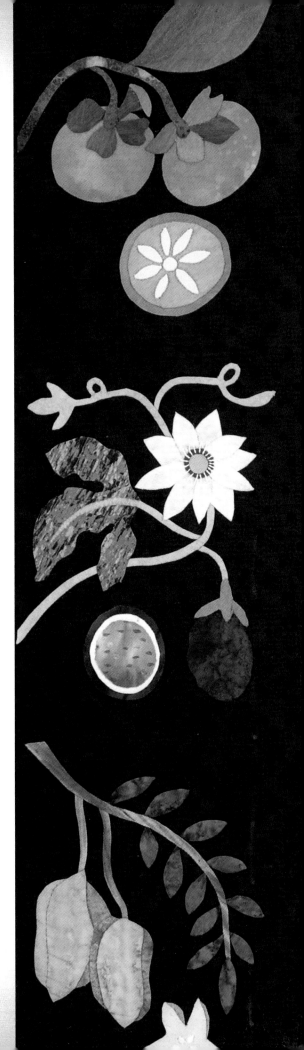

also excellent, however, the color choice is limited and it is more expensive. Any very fine thread can be used. Threads are numbered according to size: the higher the number, the finer the thread.

Thimbles: A thimble not only protects your finger, it helps you to get the desired stitch quality in your work. There are many types available, including metal, plastic and leather. There are even pads to position on your finger in place of a thimble. Be sure to try the thimble on for size: check that it is neither too tight nor will fall off your finger with every movement. I use a standard, metal thimble with dimples and with a small rim on top to keep the needle from slipping.

Pins: For appliqué, I use silk pins with glass heads. They are smooth, very sharp and thin, and do not leave holes in your fabric. The glass heads make them easy to pick up and remove from your fabric or pincushion. I sometimes use the $3/4$" appliqué pins for very small pieces. I also use those very sturdy large pins ($1 3/4$") with large yellow heads. These are used to hold the sandwich of your quilt together before it is basted, and also for blocking the finished quilt on your design wall.

Scissors: Scissors are a long-term investment and with care, they will last a lifetime. For appliqué, I use two pairs of 5" scissors with sharp points: one pair for fabric and one pair for paper. This size is convenient for cutting small pieces and the points are sharp for snipping curves and notches. My paper scissors have a bright-colored handle so I can easily tell the two apart.

Markers: There is no one perfect marking pen or pencil, and there are many different types available. What works on one fabric may not work on another. To mark my patterns on to the freezer paper, I use a mechanical pencil or a sharp pointed pencil. To mark on light background fabric, I use the .5mm super-thin-lead quilter's pencil. It is always sharp and does not smear. For dark colors, I use a white or pastel colored chalk pencil that can be sharpened to make a very thin line, and be brushed off. At times, I also use the fine-line wash-out marking pens. There are many different markers on the market and since they are not expensive, you can have an assortment. The main thing to remember is to test each one on the fabric to be used to be sure that it can be seen and will wash or brush out.

Freezer paper: I draw all of my appliqué patterns on this to iron on to the fabric. This paper is inexpensive and convenient to use. If the pattern is used in several places, the paper can be used several times.

Fabric Selection

All fabrics used in these quilts are 100% cotton. For appliqué, good quality cottons with an even weave are the easiest to work with, as they will not slip and slide like silk and polyesters. The selection of commercial fabrics in the quilt shops continues to grow and improve and almost any look can be achieved. There are hand dyed batiks of every hue and complete lines of designer's fabrics that range from traditional to oriental designs. Be creative with your colors and fabric choices for these fruit. I use good quality cotton for both the background and the appliqué for my work.

Basic Appliqué Tips

- Thoroughly wash and rinse all fabrics to be used. This will remove sizing and eliminate any bleeding that may occur. Remove the fabric from the dryer while still damp and iron it dry.

- When cutting your background, add 2" to the desired size of your finished block. If you want the finished block to be 12" x 12", cut your background squares 14" x 14". While stitching the appliqué, the block can become distorted. After the appliqué is finished, trim the block to size.

- Spray the background fabric with starch and iron it dry before you mark the pattern on it. The starch gives body to the background and keeps the background from wrinkling as you mark the pattern. With this added body, you can draw a very fine line pattern on your background.

- Center the background block over the pattern and draw the complete pattern, with your choice of marker, on this background block. If your background is dark or patterned, use a light box or window to see the pattern through the fabric.

Tip

Many of the leaf patterns have lines drawn on them. These lines can be embroidered, used as quilting lines, or deleted in your final quilt.

- Draw the appliqué patterns on the dull side of freezer paper and cut them out on the drawn line. Do not add a seam allowance to the paper patterns. Mark each pattern piece with its number. Follow this number sequence to appliqué the pieces onto the background.

- Iron the individual pattern pieces onto the right side of the desired fabrics. Mark around each piece with a marker. This is your stitching line. Cut out these appliqué pieces, leaving a 1/4" seam allowance. This seam allowance may be trimmed closer as you work on each individual piece.

- Beginning with piece 1 with the freezer paper still in place, turn the seam allowance to the back and crease the seam allowance on the sewing line around the entire piece. Remove the freezer paper and position the piece in the correct spot on the background. Secure it with a pin and slipstitch it in place. Following the numbered sequence, appliqué the remaining pieces in the same manner.

Fusible Web

There are many brands of fusible web on the market. I have used several of them and they basically all work. The important thing to remember is to follow the manufacturer's instructions for iron temperatures, time required and procedures for each brand. To avoid a backward design, the pattern must be reversed.

Finishing

- When the appliqué is finished, wash out all the markings that show. Press and trim the block to the finished size including seam allowance.

- Depending on the wallhanging or quilt that you are making, sew the individual blocks together and add the sashings and or borders (if they are needed for your particular project).

- Press the top and mark the quilting pattern.

- Cut the backing and the batting about 2" larger than the quilt top.

- Press the backing to be sure that it is smooth.

- Spread the backing, wrong side up, on a flat surface. I use my work table, or if the piece is too large, I work on the floor. Secure this piece on the flat surface with masking tape on each corner and on the sides to keep the backing smooth.

- Center the batting over the backing and smooth in place.

- Add the top, right side up, over the batting and smooth in place.

- Using those large pins with the yellow heads, I pin the entire top, batting and backing together about every 8" and around the entire edge.

- Thread-baste the entire quilt. I start in the center and first baste a horizontal row, then a vertical row. Continue in this manner, keeping the rows about 4" to 5" apart. Baste around the entire outer edge of the quilt.

- When the quilt is basted, turn the raw edges of the backing over the batting and baste. This keeps the batting from fraying on the edges as you quilt.

Blocking a Quilt

- When the quilting is finished, remove all the basting stitches. Check both the front and back side of the quilt and remove any loose threads and lint.

- Measure the quilt from side to side, top to bottom and diagonally. Pin it on your design wall, or if it is too large, on a sheet over a short-pile carpet. Use a sturdy ruler to be certain that the corners and sides are straight. Maneuver the quilt gently, but do not stretch the fabric. Pin the corners and about every 6" around the entire quilt. Be sure the quilt remains smooth and true to size.

- When the quilt is pinned and smooth, use a spray bottle with cold water and spray the entire quilt. Pat the water in to be sure that the entire quilt is evenly wet.

- Let the quilt dry completely. When it's dry, place it on your work table. Using a square ruler, trim away the excess batting, backing, and uneven edges from the quilt. After the quilt is trimmed, place it on a flat surface and measure it again to be sure all is accurate and as square as possible.

- Bind with a double-fold binding.

- After the binding is attached, measure and block again and pin around the entire edge. Spray again with cold water. Be sure that the edges are wet. This makes your binding a part of the quilt and keeps it smooth. Let it dry completely. With this method of blocking, your quilt will have a smooth surface, straight edges and no rippling. It is a little more work, but well worth it.

Citrus Wallhanging 35" x 35"

Citrus Fruits

itrus are sub-tropical evergreen plants originating in southeast Asia. The citrus are the most important fruit crop next to grapes. Citrus was first brought to the United States in the 16th century. Most of our citrus is now grown in Florida, Texas and California. Included in these patterns are five citrus fruit: grapefruit, kumquat, lemon, lime and orange.

Fabric Requirements

Fat quarters or scraps of green, yellow and orange for the fruit and leaves

Background, border and binding: $1^1/2$ yards

Sashing: $1/3$ yard

Contrast: $1/4$ yard

$1^1/4$ yards backing

Batting: 39" x 39"

How to Make This Quilt

- The lemon, lime, orange and grapefruit are appliquéd on $12^1/2$" blocks. See pages 20-21 and 24-25 for templates.

- Green accent strips were used to define the 4 blocks, but they do not change the size. To make these strips, cut 16 green strips 1" x $12^1/2$". With wrong sides together, fold these strips in half lengthwise and press. Align the edges and sew these strips to all 4 sides of the citrus blocks with a $1/8$" seam allowance.

- For the inner sashing, cut 4 sashing strips $1^1/2$" x $12^1/2$". Sew a vertical strip between the 2 top blocks and the 2 bottom fruit blocks with a $1/4$" seam allowance.

- Cut a $1^1/2$" square of the background fabric and sew to the 2 remaining sashes. Connect the top and bottom fruit with this horizontal sash and with a $1/4$" seam allowance.

- Surround these 4 fruit blocks with a 1" finished sashing strip.

- For the outer border, cut 2 background strips $4^1/2$" x $27^1/2$". Sew onto both sides.

- Cut 2 background strips $4^1/2$" x $35^1/2$" and sew onto the top and bottom.

- Appliqué kumquats and blossoms randomly on the outer border. Refer to the quilt photo for placement.

- Sandwich the top, batting and backing together and quilt as desired.

- Trim to size and bind with background fabric.

Citrus Wallhanging 35" x 35"

4"

1"

12" x 12"

Oranges

Lemons

Grapefruit

Limes

Kumquat

Assembly Diagram

Recipes

Orange Slices in Citrus Syrup

4 oranges
Zest of 1 orange

For the syrup
1 1/2 cups orange juice
2 tablespoons honey
2 tablespoons orange liqueur (optional)

• Stand the orange upright and with a sharp
  knife, cut off the peel and the white pith—
  do this for all 4 oranges. Cut the oranges
  crosswise into 1/2" slices. Place in a shallow glass bowl.
• Cut the zest from 1 orange into julienne
  strips 4" long. Place in a small saucepan,
  cover with water, and boil for 1 minute.
  Drain and set aside.
• Combine orange juice and honey in a
  medium sauce pan. Bring to a boil to dissolve
  the honey. Lower the heat and simmer until
  the mixture thickens to light syrup (about
  5 minutes). Add the orange zest to the
  syrup. Cook until the zest is translucent,
  about 3 to 5 minutes.
• Cover and refrigerate until well chilled.
  To serve, place orange slices in individual
  dishes and pour syrup over the slices.
  Drizzle each serving with 1 1/2 teaspoon
  of orange liqueur. Serves 4.

Kumquat Compote

Kumquats
Sugar
Pineapple juice

In a medium-size sauce pan, cover the unpeeled
kumquats with water and parboil for 5 minutes.
Drain and cool. Slice off the top, remove the seeds
and fill each fruit with 1/2 teaspoon sugar. Stand
upright in a shallow buttered pan. Bake about
15 minutes in a preheated 350 degree oven,
basting frequently with pineapple juice. This may
be used as a dessert, a garnish or may accompany
a meat dish.

Orange

Oranges are the most popular of the citrus fruits. Florida produces the most oranges of any state, but large quantities also come from California, Texas and Arizona. Oranges are mainly harvested in the winter, but some variety is always available in the stores. A large portion of the crop is made into juice. Ripe fruit that is heavy for its size will be the juiciest; however, size alone is not an indication of quality as larger fruit is often thick skinned.

Number of pattern pieces: 31

Fabrics needed
Fat quarters or scraps of 2 - 3 orange fabrics for the oranges, 2 - 3 green fabrics for the leaves, brown for the stems, white for the blossoms and yellow for the center.

Tip
Leave the end of leaf (13) loose until the orange (15) is in place, then appliqué the leaf down. Leave a small opening in the top of the orange. Insert the end of the stem (17) and appliqué piece (15) over it.

Lemon

To cook without lemons would be unthinkable. We use them in vinaigrettes and sauces. They add life to our vegetables and to fish and are most important in our desserts. They are grown in southern California and central and south Florida. Most lemons belong to the common varieties of the citrus lemon. They are bright yellow and oval in shape, and their yield is plentiful from late winter to early summer.

Number of pattern pieces: 16

Fabrics needed

Fat quarters or scraps of 2 - 3 yellow fabrics for the lemons, 2 - 3 green fabrics for the leaves, brown for the stems and white for the inside of the lemon.

Tip

For the cut lemon, cut a full-size pattern for the outer skin. After it is appliquéd in place, cut away the background leaving 1/4" seam allowance. Cut a full-size pattern for the white part of the lemon. Appliqué it in place, then trim away the yellow background behind it. Cut the 2 full-size patterns for the yellow part of the inside of the lemon and appliqué in place, then trim away the white background behind it. The seeds can be appliquéd or embroidered with a satin stitch.

For templates, see next page.

Orange

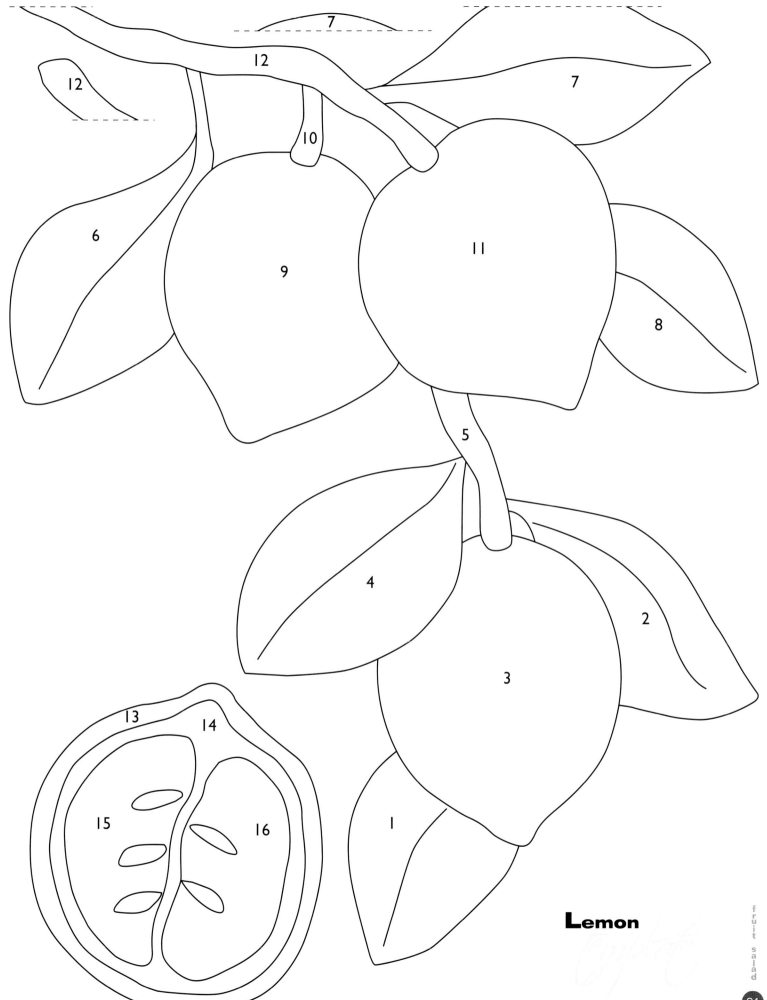

Lemon

Lime

Limes, like lemons, are too acidic to eat alone. However, a squeeze of lime juice can boost flavor and add a spicy fragrance to cooking. Two types of limes are grown in southern California and in southern Florida. The larger Tahiti or Persian lime is grown in both states and the small Key or Mexican limes are grown in Florida. Their green skin is smooth and thin. It can turn yellow when completely ripe, although the flesh always remains green.

Number of pattern pieces: 24

Fabrics needed

Fat quarters or scraps of green fabrics for the limes and leaves, brown for the stems. To distinguish between the limes and the leaves, choose 2 - 3 shades of a lime or lighter green for the fruit, and 2 - 3 shades of a medium to darker green for the leaves.

Grapefruit

The grapefruit is somewhat of a newcomer in the citrus family. It is the refined descendant of a bigger and rougher fruit, the pomelo. The grapefruit was introduced to Florida in the early part of the 19th century and later cultivation spread to Texas, California and Arizona. Grapefruit season is mainly from October to June, but they can be found in the markets year-round. Look for smooth and glossy skin and fruit that is heavy for its size. About half of the world crop is made into juice, but a half grapefruit at the breakfast table or segments in your dinner salad are most rewarding.

Number of pattern pieces: 24

Fabrics needed

Fat quarters or scraps of a yellow-green fabric for the grapefruit, 2 green fabrics for the leaves, white for the flowers and cut piece of fruit, and yellow for the flower centers.

Tip

For the cut grapefruit, cut a full size circle for piece 18 and appliqué it in place. Trim away the background fabric, leaving a $1/4$" seam allowance. Then cut a circle of white fabric for piece 19 and appliqué it in place. Trim away the background fabric, leaving a $1/4$" seam allowance. For piece 20, cut in one piece and appliqué it in place, then mark the segments with a quilting line, or cut the individual segments and appliqué into place. The seeds can be appliquéd or embroidered with the satin stitch.

For templates, see next page.

Lime
template

24

Grapefruit

Recipes

Blueberry Spinach Salad

1 lb. of fresh spinach
1 1/2 cups fresh or frozen blueberries, thawed
4 oz. blue cheese crumbles
1/2 cup toasted pecans

Salad Dressing
1/2 cup vegetable oil
3 tablespoons white wine vinegar
1 teaspoon Dijon mustard
Salt to taste

Combine the torn fresh spinach, blueberries, blue cheese and pecans in a salad bowl. Toss the greens and the salad dressing gently, serve immediately. Serves 4.

Strawberries Romanoff

1 quart strawberries sugared
and cut into quarters
1 pint vanilla ice cream
1/2 cup heavy cream

3 tablespoons Cointreau liqueur

Place the sugared strawberries in glass bowl. Soften ice cream and whip slightly. Whip heavy cream and fold into the ice cream. Add Cointreau. Blend the cream and the strawberries together gently with a spoon and serve immediately. Serves 4.

1

2

13

7

5

3

8

6

4

9

11

12

10

14

Kumquat

Berries Wallhanging 33" x 33"

Berries

Berries of many varieties are grown in the United States. They are a small-sized, pulpy fruit. Some are used only for jams and jelly, but most are eaten fresh from the vine or plant. Included are the blueberry, gooseberry, raspberry and the strawberry.

Fabric Requirements

Fat quarters or scraps of green for the leaves and assorted colors for the berries
Background: 1 yard
Border and binding: $1^1/2$ yards
Contrast border: $^1/4$ yard
$1^1/4$ yards backing
Batting: 37" x 37"

How to Make This Quilt

- Cut a 33" square of background fabric. Mark the scallop pattern on this background (see Assembly Diagram, page 33). To do this, mark the center of each side and place a mark 3" from each edge. On the 4 corners, with a marker, mark a 45° line 7" from each corner toward the center and place a mark 7" from each corner. Place the scallop pattern on these 2 marks: the center on the 3" mark and on the corner 7" mark. Draw the scallop pattern onto the background with a marker. Reverse the scallop and mark from the corner to the next side. Make certain that the centers are all 3" from the edge and the corners are 7" from the corner. Continue marking the scallop around the entire background.

- Mark the patterns for the 4 berries on the background inside the scalloped border.

- After the appliqué for the berries is finished, cut away the outer edges of the background fabric following the scallop pattern, leaving a $^1/4$" seam allowance.

- Center this scalloped background on a 34" square of border fabric. In the seam allowance, baste the background onto the border fabric. Turn it to the back side and cut away the excess border fabric under the background.

- To cover the raw edges, cut 8 pieces of contrast border fabric on the bias 1" wide x 13" long. Turn under a $^1/4$" seam allowance on either side and slip stitch it in place over the raw edges. Trim as needed in the corners and miter these corners for a neat finish.

- Sandwich the top, batting and backing together and quilt as desired.

- Trim to size and bind with border fabric.

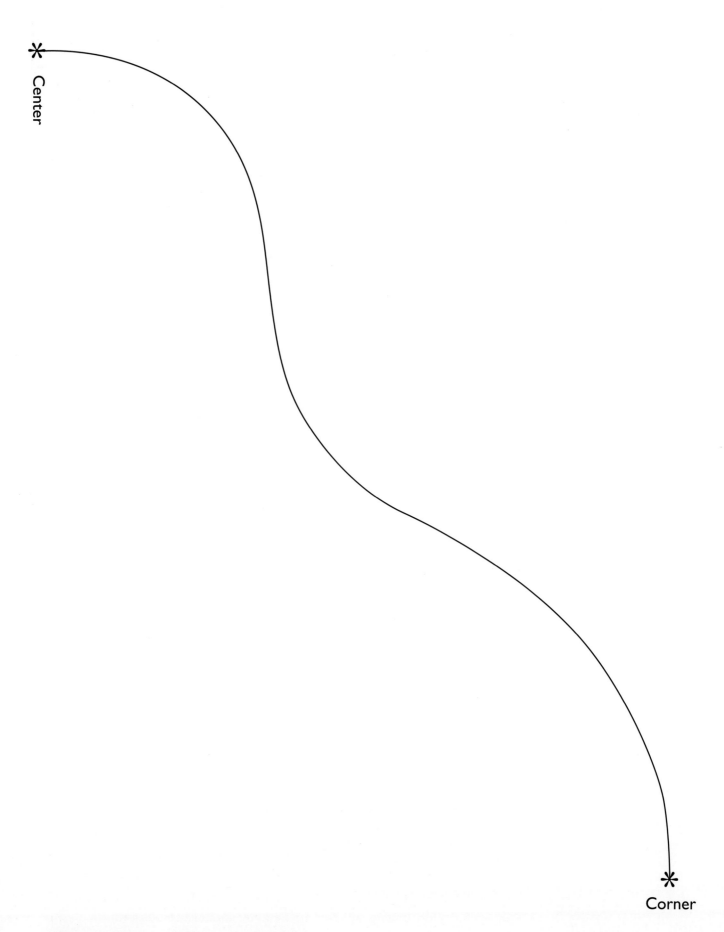

Center

Corner

Border Template

Berries 33" x 33"

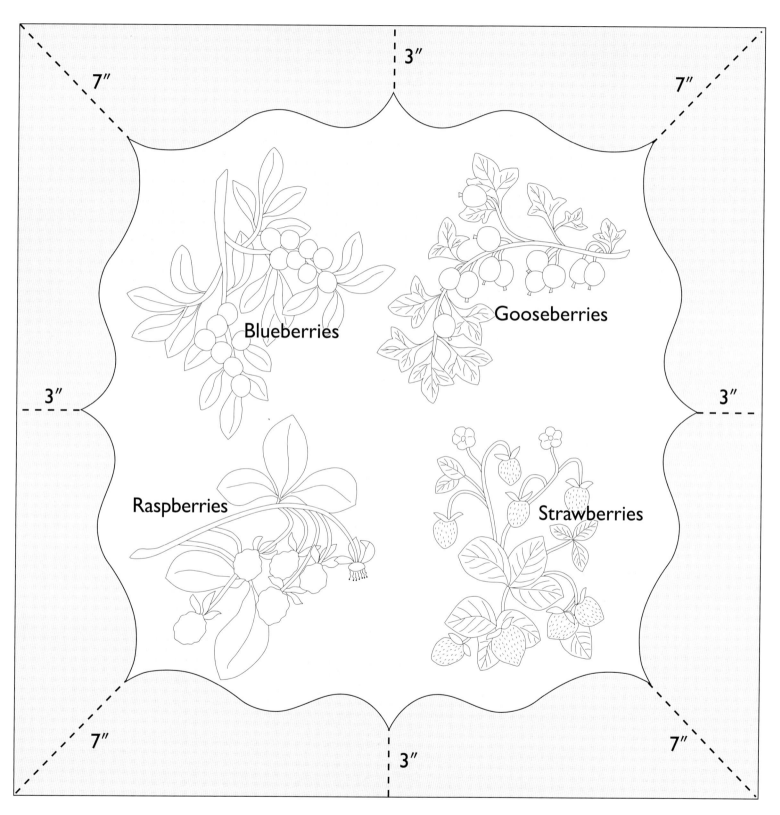

Assembly Diagram

$\mathcal{W}$ild blueberries are widespread throughout the central and eastern parts of North America, the largest producers of blueberries. They were first cultivated in southern New Jersey. The blueberry was an important source of food for Native Americans: eaten fresh in the summer, and dried in the sun for use in the winter. The blueberry season starts in May in the South and moves north and west where the season lasts from July until early September.

Number of pattern pieces: 38

Fabrics needed

Fat quarters or scraps of several shades of deep blue for the blueberries; several shades of medium green fabric for the leaves, and brown for the branches.

Gooseberries

Gooseberries were first cultivated in Britain. The berries were mainly grown and used for desserts, however when picked under-ripe, they can be used in sauces for fish and some poultry. There are several kinds of gooseberries: white, yellow, red, and purple, as well as green.

Number of pattern pieces: 37

Fabrics needed

Fat quarters or scraps can be used. Several shades of medium green fabrics were used for the leaves. The color of the gooseberries will be your choice. Choose several shades of a color that will contrast with your background fabric. The calyx at the bottom of the fruit can be drawn with a permanent marker or embroidered with the stem stitch using 2 strands of embroidery floss.

For templates, see next page.

Blueberries

Gooseberries

Raspberries

Raspberries are one of the most coveted and popular of the summer fruits. Wild raspberries grow all across North America. Cultivated raspberries now are also grown across North America. The season begins in May in the South and generally ends as late as July in the cooler states. The berries are very fragile and cannot be stored for any length of time.

Number of pattern pieces: 34

Fabrics needed

Fat quarters or scraps can be used. The blossom is white, the raspberries are a raspberry red and the leaves are a medium green. The stamens were embroidered with two strands of gold colored floss.

Strawberries can be grown anywhere in the United States. California produces 80 percent of the commercially grown strawberries, and Florida is the second-largest producer. Strawberries are fragile when ripe, so they are picked before they reach full maturity. Since they can be grown in all 50 states, look for these berries at your local stores and farmer's markets. Perfectly ripe strawberries are best eaten raw, sliced with fresh cream and sugar or made into the classic strawberry shortcake or into jams.

Number of pattern pieces: 42

Fabrics needed

Fat quarters or scraps can be used. The flowers are white with yellow in the center, the berries bright red, and the leaves medium green.

Tip

Leaves on the strawberries are numbered as one piece - they can be cut out together or separately. Flower centers may be appliquéd or embroidered.

For templates, see next page.

Raspberries

40

Strawberries

fruit salad

41

Exotic Fruits Wallhanging 41" x 47"

These exotic fruits are not widely known as they grow only in tropical climates or in other countries. However, with our global economy they are now being introduced throughout our country. I have included nine fruits: carambola or star fruit, fig, guava, mango, papaya, passion fruit, persimmon, pomegranate and monstera deliciosa.

Fabric Requirements

Fat quarters or scraps in a wide variety of colors, refer to the 9 individual fruit instructions

Background and outer border: 2 yards

First border: $1/4$ yard

Second border: $1/4$ yard

Third border and binding: 1 yard

$1 1/2$ yards backing

Batting: 45" x 51"/crib size

How to Make This Quilt

- Appliqué the 9 fruit on 12" x 14" blocks. These will be trimmed to the correct size when finished.

- When the appliqué is finished, trim each block to 10" x 12", *plus seam allowance.*

- Sew the blocks together 3 across and 3 down for the center of the quilt.

- **First border:** For a finished $3/4$" border, cut 2 strips $1 1/4$" wide x $36 1/2$" long and sew onto the sides. Cut 2 strips $1 1/4$" wide x 32" long and sew to the top and bottom.

- **Second border:** For a finished $3/4$" border, cut 2 strips $1 1/4$" wide x 38" long and sew onto the sides. Cut 2 strips $1 1/4$" wide x 33 1/2" long and sew onto the top and bottom.

- **Third border:** For a finished 1" border, cut 2 strips $1 1/2$" wide x $39 1/2$" long and sew onto the sides. Cut 2 strips $1 1/2$" wide x $35 1/2$" long and sew onto the top and bottom.

- **Outer border:** From the background fabric for a finished 3" border, cut 2 strips 3 $1/2$" wide x $41 1/2$" long and sew onto the sides. Cut 2 strips $3 1/2$" wide x $41 1/2$" long and sew onto the top and bottom.

- Mark the quilting design you desire, then layer the top, batting and backing.

- After the quilting is finished, bind with a $1/2$" binding. To make this, cut the binding fabric 3" wide. Fold it in half with wrong sides together and press. With raw edges matching, sew this binding onto the right side of the quilt with a $1/2$" seam allowance. Turn it to the back and slipstitch in place.

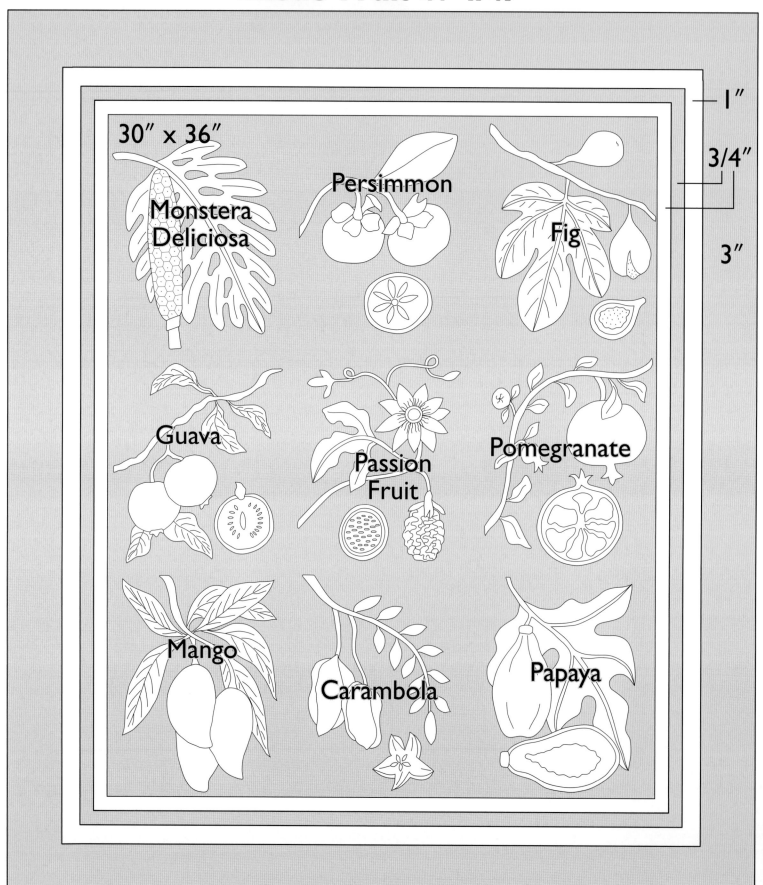

30" x 36"

Monstera Deliciosa

Persimmon

Fig

1"

3/4"

3"

Guava

Passion Fruit

Pomegranate

Mango

Carambola

Papaya

Assembly Diagram

Recipes

Waldorf Salad

2 crisp apples, 1 red and 1 green
Juice of 1 lemon
1 cup chopped celery
$1/2$ cup chopped walnuts, slightly toasted
$1/2$ cup mayonnaise
Salt and pepper to taste

Core and dice the apples (leave the skin on).
You need about 2 cups. Toss the apples in the
lemon juice. Add the chopped celery and the
toasted walnuts. Add the mayonnaise to bind
the mixture and season with salt and pepper.
Serve on lettuce leaves. Serves 4.

Kiwi Sauce

1 cup kiwi puree (made from $2/3$ pound of
peeled and stemmed fruit)
3 tablespoons sugar, or to taste

Peel the kiwi and cut out the hard stem at one end.
Chop the flesh coarsely and puree it in a food processor.
Stir in the sugar, it will dissolve in about 10 minutes.
The sauce can be made ahead, covered and chilled.
Makes about 1 cup. Kiwi sauce goes well with custard,
pound cake or overripe sliced bananas.

Stuffed Pears

4 pears
$1/2$ cup raisins
2 tablespoons chopped walnuts
2 tablespoons sugar
1 tablespoon lemon juice
$1/2$ cup light corn syrup

Pear, core and halve 4 firm pears. Place in a
baking dish with 2 tablespoons water. Mix together raisins, sugar, walnuts and lemon juice
and fill the pear hollows. Pour the light corn
syrup over them. Cover and bake until tender, about 30 minutes in a 350 degree oven.
Serves 4.

This is a most exotic fruit and not well known in the United States. It is native to Mexico and Guatemala. I include this fruit because I spent my childhood in Miami and we had a monstera deliciosa plant on our patio wall. This plant is a member of the arum lily family and is grown in the United States as a houseplant. It is sometimes called the Swiss cheese plant because of its very large scalloped leaves with natural holes in them. The holes permit rain to reach the roots and reduce resistance to strong tropical winds. The fruit takes just over a year to ripen. Ripe fruit are about 12" long and about 4-5" in circumference. The flesh is very sweet and tastes like pineapple, banana, and mango. It can be eaten plain, as a dessert, or in salads.

Number of pattern pieces: 9

Fabrics needed

Fat quarters or scraps can be used. A deep green was used for the vein and a medium batik green was used for the 8 1/2" x 10 1/2" leaf. A geometric print of a dull gold or a golden yellow is used for the fruit skin, which is similar to the pineapple but not as rough. Use a medium brown for the fruit stem.

Tip

Baste the vein in place first—appliqué leaf pieces 2 - 6 over the vein. The section of vein above the leaf was slip stitched in place. After the outer edges of the leaf are appliquéd, turn the edges of the holes under and appliqué them. Tuck the edge of piece 9 under piece 8 when appliquéing.

ersimmons that grow in America originated in China and were known as kaki. The American persimmon is grown in the southern parts of the United States, from the Carolinas west to California. The persimmon tree is more like a bush and grows about six feet in height. The leaves are dark and lustrous, the flowers are drab, and the fruit is pink to orange to red in color and about three inches in diameter. Persimmon are sometimes described as looking like large orange tomatoes. They should be eaten only when soft and somewhat shriveled, as unripe persimmons are mouth-puckering. Eat persimmons fresh, dried, or candied.

Number of pattern pieces: 24

Fabrics needed

Fat quarters or scraps can be used. Dark green was used for the leaves, brown for the stem and light reddish orange for the fruit and white for the seeds.

Tip

After you appliqué piece 15 in place, cut away the background before you piece 16. The seeds and center 24 were appliquéd, but can be embroidered with white floss if desired.

For templates, see next page.

Monstera
Deliciosa

48

Persimmon

1

3 4

8

7

5

6

13

14

10

12

11

9

2

19 18

20

24

17

21

23

16

22

15

Fig

igs have been grown around the Mediterranean in Greece and southern Europe since B.C. Figs in this country were first planted by Spanish missionaries in California. Although they are now grown in our warmer states, most of our figs still come from California. The tree is very bushy and can be trimmed as a tree, a bush or trained on walls. It can grow as tall as 30 feet. The leaves are large and distinctive and the fruit is pear-shaped and grows between 2" - 4" long. Depending on the variety, figs can be brown, green or deep purple. They are delicious fresh, but are extremely perishable, so we are most familiar with the dried fruit.

Number of pattern pieces: 14

Fabrics needed

Fat quarters or scraps can be used. Two shades of green were used for the leaf, and brown for the stem. A mottled purple and green batik was used for the figs, and red for the flesh.

Tips

To achieve the narrow veins, cut the web of the veins in one piece from the light green fabric. Add a seam allowance to this web and baste it to the background in the seam allowance. The leaf is divided into 6 sections. Appliqué these sections (2 - 7) with the dark green fabric over the veins. For the cross section of the fig, appliqué piece 12 first and cut away the background from the back. As you appliqué pieces 13 and 14, cut away the backgrounds to eliminate the extra bulk.

The guava is native to South America, but was cultivated in other tropical areas. It is also grown in Hawaii, southern California, and southern Florida. Guava trees are small, almost like a spreading shrub. The leaves are thick and leathery and the flowers are rather insignificant. The fruit ranges from plum- to apple-sized and are mostly round in shape. The skin is thin and smooth and the color can be greenish-yellow or a pale red. The flesh is light red in color and filled with seeds which can be eaten. Guavas are very sweet and best eaten fresh off the tree. They are also used cooked and raw in desserts, and made into jelly.

Number of pattern pieces: 14

Guava

Fabrics needed

Fat quarters or scraps can be used. Mottled green was used for the leaves, brown for the branch, yellow for the guavas and pale red for the flesh.

Tip

I reverse appliquéd the center of the guava cross-section. The seeds were painted on with a permanent fabric marker.

For templates, see next page.

Fig

2

11

3

5

1

4

6

9

7

8

10

11

13

12

14

52

Guava

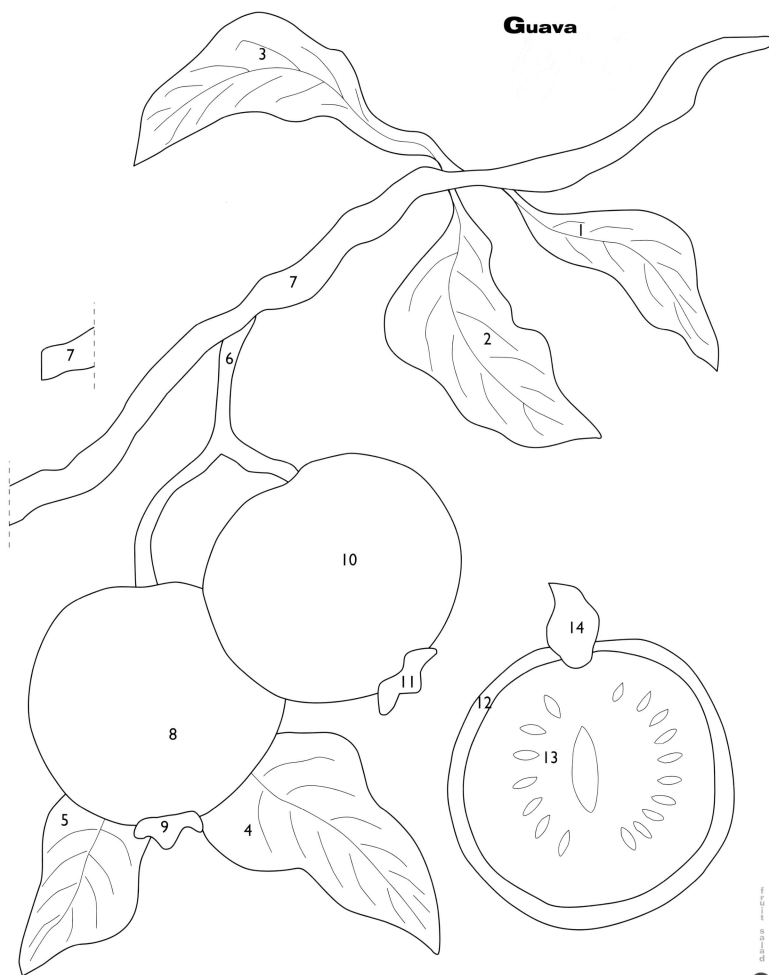

Passion Fruit

Passion fruit grows on a perennial vine with large deeply-lobed leaves, spectacular flowers, and peculiar fruit. The plant is native to Brazil, but since the 19th century has been grown in Australia, New Zealand and Hawaii. These plants, with their delightful flowers and delicious fruits, have become popular in all warm climates and are often grown on patios for the lovely flowers. The fruit is about the size of a hen's egg. It has a brittle outer shell, which is wrinkled when ripe. The pulp is soft and yellow-orange, and filled with seeds that can be eaten. The flavor is sweet and strong–passion fruit can be eaten plain or used in ice cream and sherbets.

Number of pattern pieces: 25

Fabrics needed

Fat quarters or scraps can be used. I used 2 shades of green for the leaf and vine, deep purple for the fruit, white for the flower, purple and gold for its center and a golden orange for the pulp.

Tip

Vein 3 was appliquéd before leaf 10. I cut the leaf apart and appliquéd it onto the vein in 2 parts. Cut a full circle for piece 23 and after it is appliquéd, cut away the background. Appliqué pieces 24 and 25 in the same manner. The stamens were embroidered with white floss.

The word pomegranate means *apple with many seeds,* and when you cut through the leathery skin, you will find an interior of surprising beauty. Pomegranates are filled with clusters of juicy red seeds, separated by creamy white membranes. The cultivation of this fruit predates written history. It probably originated in southwestern Asia, but is now grown worldwide in hot, dry climates. Most of our commercially grown fruit comes from the central valley of California. Pomegranates grow on large bushes or small trees, covered with brilliant flowers in the spring. The fruit is about the size of a softball and is deep red in color. Pomegranates can be eaten fresh, dried or candied. The seeds can be added to salads or desserts and the juice is delicious.

Number of pattern pieces: 28

Fabrics needed

Fat quarters or scraps can be used. One medium green fabric was used for the leaves, bright pink or light red for the flowers, deep red for the pomegranate, and creamy white for the membrane.

Tip

Appliqué leaf 4 under stem 5, but leave the leaf free until branch 19 is in place. For the cross-section of the pomegranate, appliqué piece 20 first and cut away the background. Appliqué the membrane piece 21 and cut away the red background. Appliqué the seed clusters onto piece 21.

For templates, see next page.

Passion Fruit

Pomegranate

The mango is one of the most delicious of the tropical fruits. It is a native of India, but is now grown in warm climates. Of the 50 states, only Hawaii and Florida have weather warm enough to grow mangos for market. The tree is medium to large, with masses of rich green narrow leaves. Depending on the variety, the fruit comes in various shapes—round, oblong or kidney-shaped—and weigh from about a half-pound to a couple of pounds. Mangos soften as they ripen. The skin can be yellow, orange, or red, and the flesh ranges from pale yellow to deep orange. Mangos can be eaten raw or made into jams, chutneys, pickles or preserves.

Mango

Number of pattern pieces: 11

Fabrics needed

Fat quarters or scraps can be used. Use 2-3 green fabrics to distinguish between the leaves and 2-3 different shades of your choice of color for the mangos to distinguish between them.

Carambola Star Fruit

Carambolas, also called star fruit, are native to Indonesia but because of their hardiness and decorative values, they are now grown in many tropical countries and in the United States in zone 10. The trees are small and delicate. The fruit is yellow, about 5" long, with five prominent ridges running the length so that the cross section resembles a star. The skin has a waxy feel to it and the flesh is juicy when ripe. In the United States, star fruit are used as garnish. They can be eaten plain if picked ripe, used in salads or made into jam.

Number of pattern pieces: 26

Fabrics needed

Fat quarters or scraps can be used. I used a mottled batik for the leaves and brown for the stems. Three shades of gold were used to distinguish the ridges of the fruit and to distinguish the skin from the flesh in the cross-section. The seeds in the cross-section of the fruit were embroidered with white floss.

For templates, see next page.

Mango

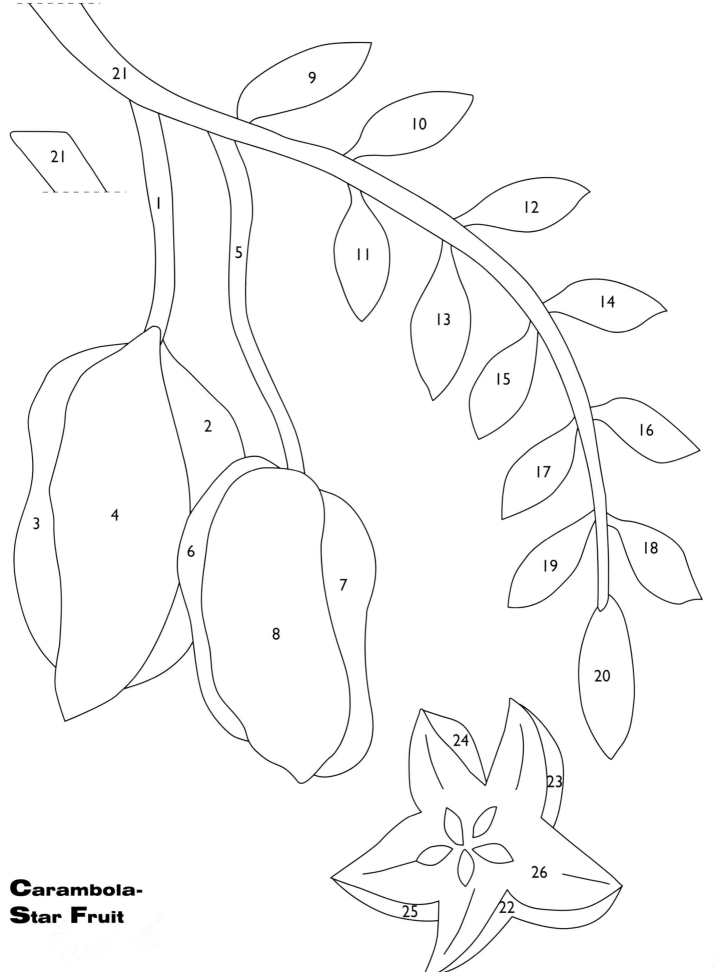

**Carambola-
Star Fruit**

Recipes

Persimmon Salad with Pomegranates and Walnuts

2 ripe persimmons
$1/4$ cup pomegranate seeds
$1/4$ cup walnuts
1 tablespoon sherry vinegar
2 tablespoons extra-virgin olive oil
Salt and pepper

Peel and cut the persimmon into quarters and remove seeds. Slice the quarters into thin wedges. Toast the walnuts in the oven for 6 minutes or in a non-stick fry pan over medium heat.

Make vinaigrette by mixing vinegar with $1/4$ teaspoon salt and a few grinds of pepper. Whisk in the olive oil. Mix persimmons, walnuts and pomegranate seeds in a bowl, toss in vinaigrette and serve over Belgian endive or lettuce. Serves 2.

Papaya and Orange Fruit Cup

1 medium-to-large or 2 small fully-ripe papaya
2 oranges

Peel and remove the seeds of the papaya and cut into 1" pieces. Place in a glass bowl. Squeeze the oranges over the papaya, include the pulp. Cover and refrigerate up to 3 hours. Remove 30 minutes before serving. Serve papaya with orange juice in individual dishes. Serves 4.

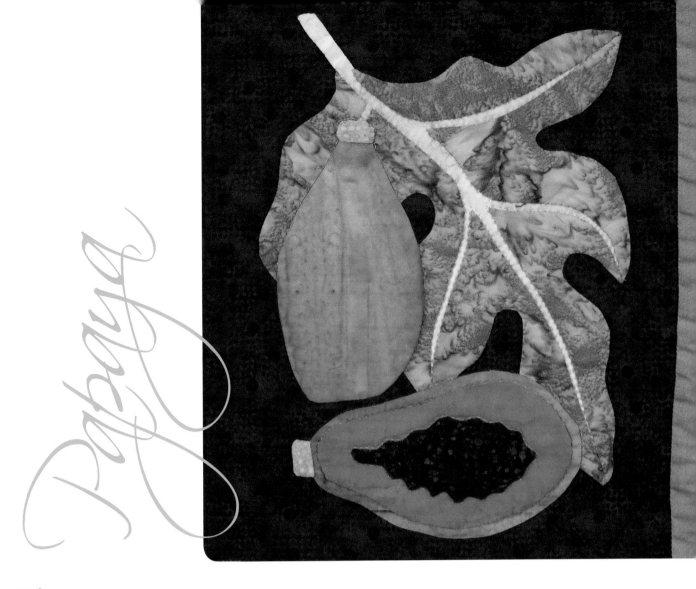

The papaya is one of the best tropical fruits. It is native to Central America, but is also grown in warm climates and in south Florida. The trees resemble palms as they are unbranched and have large big-fingered leaves. The fruit weigh between 1 to 3 pounds and is pear shaped. When ripe, it is mostly yellow orange in color. The flesh is a deeper orange, with a mass of black seeds in the center. These seeds are edible, but mostly are discarded. The flesh needs no cooking and the fruit is used in salads or for dessert after a rich meal. It is delicious seasoned with lime or orange juice.

Number of pattern pieces: 13

Fabrics needed

Fat quarters or scraps can be used. Choose 2 shades of green for the leaf, golden orange for the papaya, a deeper orange for the flesh, and black for the seeds.

Tip

I cut the vein for the leaf from one piece. I added the seam allowance and basted it in place on the background fabric. I needle-turned the top part of the vein (above the leaf) onto the background. The leaf pieces (2-7) were appliquéd individually on top of the veins. For the cross-section of the papaya, appliqué piece 10 first and cut away the background fabric. Do the same with pieces 11 and 12.

For templates, see next page.

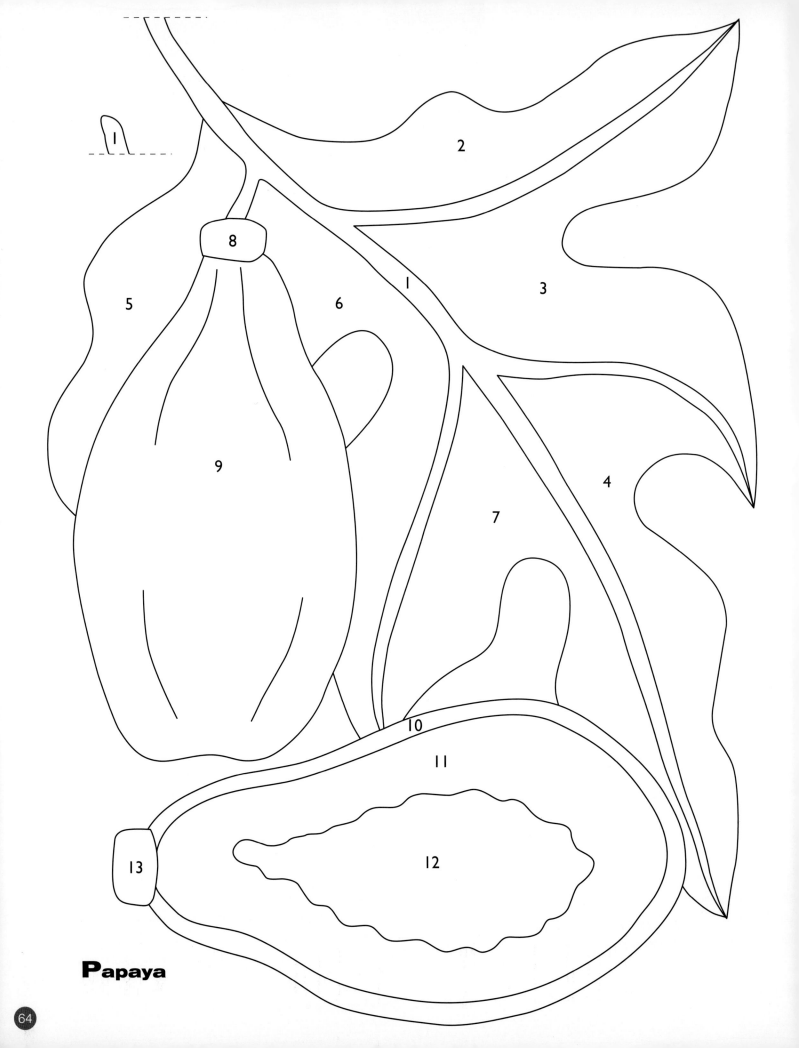

Papaya

Recipes

Baked Black Mission Figs
with Ice Cream

4 figs
1 tablespoon sugar
Sweet red wine
Ice cream

Cut the figs in half vertically and arrange them cut-side up in a buttered ceramic baking dish just large enough to hold them. Sprinkle the figs with a tablespoon of sugar and a sweet red wine. Bake in a 400 degree oven for 15 minutes. Serve warm with vanilla ice cream. Use the drippings in the baking dish as a sauce over the ice cream. Serves 2.

Star Fruit Salad

1 sliced, seeded star fruit
1 banana
Juice of 1 lime
1 orange, peeled and sliced

Mix fruits with lime juice. Cover and refrigerate until well-chilled. Serve over lettuce. Serves 2.

fruit salad

$\mathcal{I}$ call these nine fruits the common or ordinary fruits. These are the basic fruits that are in our market baskets and on our table year-around. All of these fruits are grown in the United States–perhaps in your own backyard. They are all common in our farmer's markets in season and not a month goes by in which we are unable to enjoy one or more of these fruit. I have included apples, cherries, grapes, kiwi, melon, peaches, pears, pineapple and plums.

Fabric Requirements

Fat quarters or scraps of green fabric for the leaves and assorted colors for the fruit (see individual patterns)

Background: $2^1/2$ yards

Sashing and binding: $1^1/2$ yards

$3^1/4$ yards backing

Batting: 34" x 67"/twin size

How to Make This Quilt

To make this design work, the fruit blocks are of different sizes. Before you cut the background of these various fruits, check the finished size on the Assembly Diagram and also in the tips of each of the individual fruit patterns. These fruit can be created on individual blocks in the size that you desire, but for this wallhanging, the background blocks are of different sizes. After the appliqué of the blocks is finished, trim each block to size plus seam allowance and assemble together in this manner:

The apple and the peach blocks are appliqued on $10^1/2$" x 12" finished blocks.

- Cut a $1^1/2$" x $12^1/2$" strip of the sashing fabric and sew between the apple block and the peach block.

The grapes were appliquéd on a 22" x 12" finished block.

- Cut a $1^1/2$" x $22^1/2$" strip of sashing fabric and sew onto the top of the grape block. Sew the apples and peaches block onto the grape block.

Common Fruit Wallhanging 50" x 63"

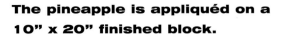

The pineapple is appliquéd on a 10" x 20" finished block.

- Cut a $1^1/2$" x $20^1/2$" strip of sashing fabric and sew onto the side of the pineapple block.

- Cut a $1^1/2$" x $11^1/2$" strip of sashing fabric and sew onto the top of the pineapple block.

- Cut a $4^1/2$" x $21^1/2$" piece from the background fabric and sew onto the sashed side of the pineapple block.

- Cut a $4^1/2$" x $15^1/2$" piece from the background fabric and sew onto the top of the pineapple block.

- Cut a $1^1/2$" x $25^1/2$" strip of sashing fabric and connect the pineapple section to the grape, apple and peach section.

The cherries, pears and plums are each appliquéd on 12" finished blocks.

- Cut 2 strips of sashing $1^1/2$" x $12^1/2$" and sew between the cherries and pears and between the pears and plums.

- Cut a $1^1/2$" x $38^1/2$" strip of sashing and sew onto the top of these 3 fruit and connect to the bottom of the pineapple and grape section.

The kiwi is appliquéd on a 12" finished block.

The melon is appliquéd on a 25" x 12" finished block.

- Cut a $1^1/2$" x $12^1/2$" strip of sashing and sew between the kiwi and the melon blocks.

- Cut a $1^1/2$" x $38^1/2$" strip of sashing fabric and sew onto the top of the kiwi and melon blocks and connect to the bottom of the cherry, pear and plum blocks.

- Cut 2 strips of sashing $1^1/2$" $51^1/2$" and sew onto the sides of the wall hanging.

- Cut 2 strips of sashing $1^1/2$" x $40^1/2$" and sew onto the top and bottom.

- From the background fabric, cut 2 pieces $4^1/2$" x $53^1/2$" and sew onto the sides.

- From the background fabric, cut 2 pieces $4^1/2$" x $48^1/2$" and sew onto the top and bottom.

- From the sashing fabric, cut 2 strips $1^1/2$" x $61^1/2$" and sew onto the sides. Cut 2 strips $1 1/2$" x $50 1/2$" and sew onto the top and bottom.

*F*or the flowering branch, cut a true bias about 2 yards total in length and $1^1/4$" wide. Fold it in half with the wrong sides together and press, and then fold the raw edges to the back. Appliqué the branches in a freeform design in the border and onto the background fabric surrounding the pineapple. Appliqué the small branches first, and then the main branch over their raw edges. There are 4 different size leaves which can be randomly appliquéd onto the vine. Insert the raw edges of these leaves under the branch. The 12 flowers which are appliquéd at the end of the branches are all the same pattern, but different shades of pink.

Sandwich the top, batting and backing together and quilt as desired.
Trim to size and bind the wallhanging with the sashing fabric.

Common Fruit
50" x 63"

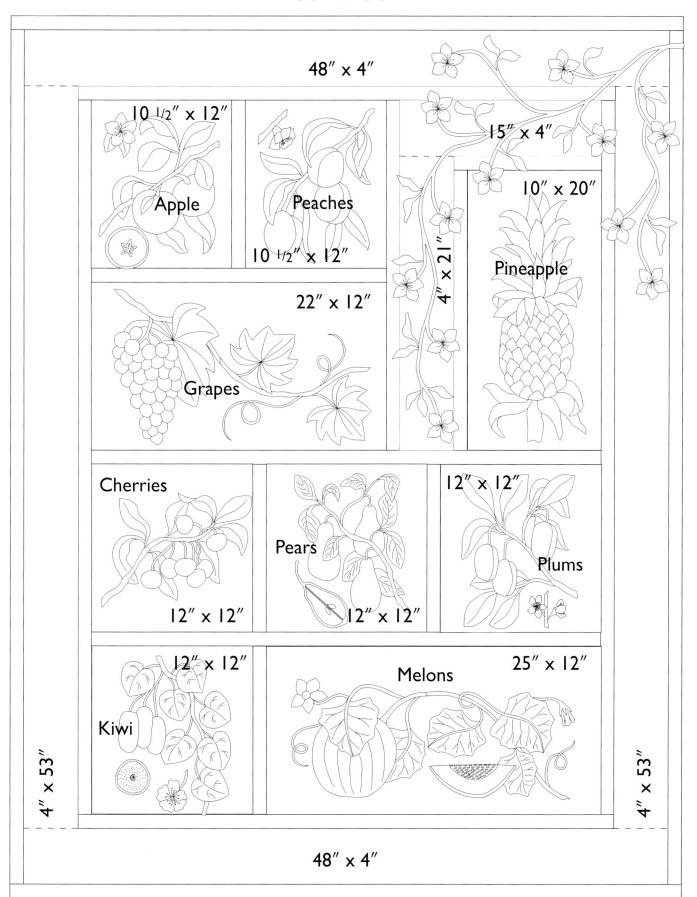

48" x 4"

15" x 4"

10 ½" x 12"
Apple

Peaches
10 ½" x 12"

10" x 20"
Pineapple

4" x 21"

22" x 12"
Grapes

Cherries

Pears

12" x 12"
Plums

12" x 12"

12" x 12"

12" x 12"

Kiwi

25" x 12"
Melons

4" x 53"

4" x 53"

48" x 4"

Assembly Diagram
Note: all inner borders and outer border are 1" wide (finished).

fruit salad

69

The apple, one of the first cultivated fruits, is now one of the most important fruits in Europe and North America. There are more than 7,000 named varieties, grown in every one of the continental United States and in 36 states on a commercial scale. The red delicious apple is the best known, but many orchards are now planting an assortment of tastier varieties. Depending on the variety, apples can be green, yellow, pink, orange, dark red to almost purple. The texture can be crisp to soft, and they may be juicy or dry. The apple harvest starts in the late summer through fall, and apples can be stored through spring. Apples can be eaten fresh off the tree, and used in salads and desserts. They can be juiced, dried, made into cider or vinegar and made into jellies.

Number of pattern pieces: 24

Fabrics needed

Fat quarters or scraps can be used. Medium green fabric was used for the leaves, red for the apples, pale pink for the blossoms and off-white for the flesh.

Tip

The apples were appliquéd on a 10$^{1}/_{2}$" x 12" finished block. Leave the top section the apple piece 12 loose until the branch piece 15 is appliquéd into place. The core and the seeds of the apple in piece 24 are embroidered with 2 strands of floss using the stem stitch.

Peach

Peaches are said to be the most widely recognized of all fruits. Peaches are of Chinese origin and they are mentioned in the book of Confucius from the first century BC. The peach came from England to North America in the 17th century. They are grown in 30 of our states, but most are grown in California, South Carolina, Georgia and Texas. The trees are small with long leaves. They bloom before the leaves appear. The peach has a partition line that makes it easy to split. The flesh may vary from near white to yellow to dark peach to almost red. The peak of the season is July and August. A perfect peach is said to be a perfect dessert. They can be eaten plain, in pies, ice cream, jams and in the famous dessert, Peach Melba.

Number of pattern pieces: 20

Fabrics needed

Fat quarters or scraps can be used. A peach-colored batik was used for the peaches and 2 shades of green for the leaves. The stem is brown. The peach blossom can be white or light or dark peach.

Tip

The peaches were appliquéd on a 10$\frac{1}{2}$" x 12" finished block. Leave the tips of leaf pieces 3 and 7 free until the peaches are appliquéd, then appliqué the tips.

For templates, see next page.

Apple

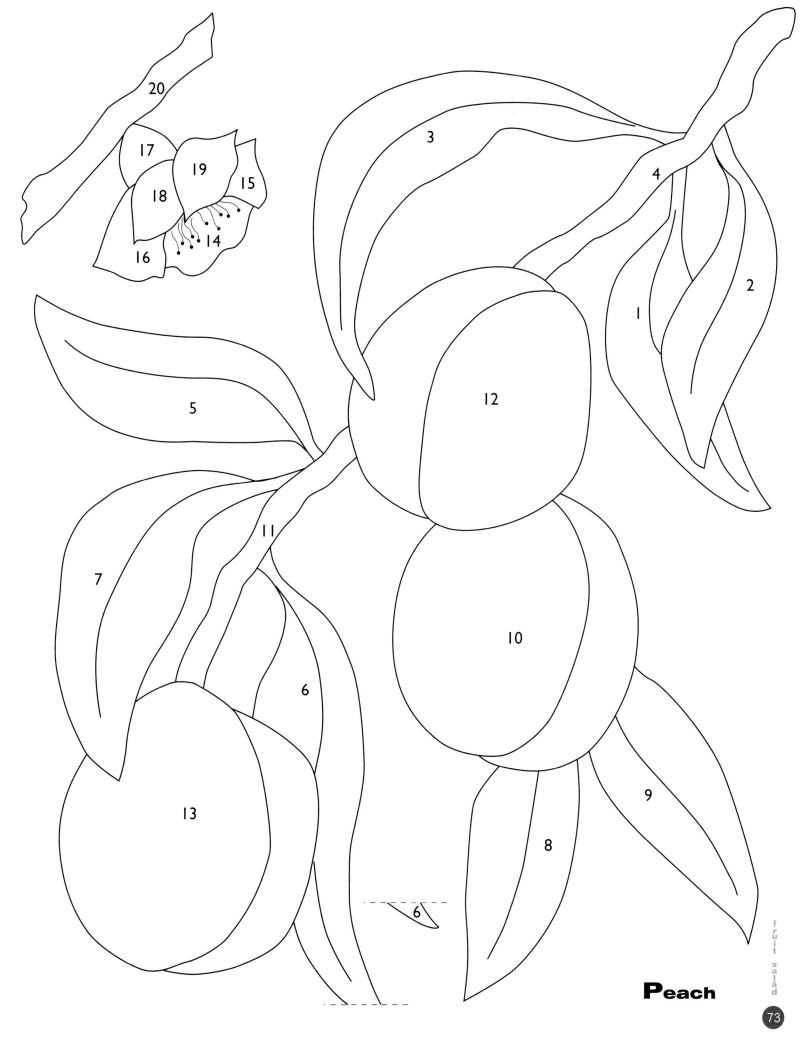

Peach

fruit salad

73

Recipes

Peach Melba

4 peaches
3 tablespoons sugar
1 quart vanilla ice cream
Raspberry coulis *(see recipe for this below)*

Peel the peaches and slice into a medium-size bowl. Toss with sugar. Cover bowl and let stand until the sugar dissolves, about 10 minutes.

To serve, place ice cream in each individual bowl. Drizzle 3 tablespoons raspberry coulis over the ice cream and top with peaches. Drizzle another tablespoon of raspberry coulis over the peaches. Serve immediately. Serves 4.

Raspberry Coulis

2 cups raspberries
1/4 cup sugar
1/4 teaspoon framboise or kirsch (optional)

Puree raspberries, sugar and framboise or kirsch together. Push the puree through a fine mesh strainer with a rubber spatula. Cover and refrigerate. Use within 3 days. *Note:* Frozen raspberries can be substituted. Thaw and push through a strainer to remove the seeds. Taste and add sugar if needed.

Pineapple

Pineapples are the most distinctive of fruits and the most popular of all tropical fruits grown in hot regions around the world. The plant resembles the common garden yuccas. The fruit grows on a central short stem on a low plant with large pointed leaves. The skin is usually gold with a tessellated appearance, but could be green depending on the variety. Most of our commercial pineapples come from Hawaii, but they are also grown in Puerto Rico and South America. Pineapples can be eaten raw and used in salads or desserts. They make delicious juice, jams, tarts, and cakes and are added to many savory main dishes.

Number of pattern pieces: 79

56 appliqué pieces for the pineapple and bottom leaves, 23 appliqué pieces for the top leaves

Fabrics needed

Fat quarters or scraps can be used. Five different green fabrics were used for the leaves. I used light and dark gold fabrics for the pineapple and put the lighter shades on the top and the darker near the base.

Tip

The pineapple was appliquéd on a 10" x 20" finished block. If you want to use only one 12" block, eliminate all the top leaves except for 19-23. Another short cut that can be taken is to use one fabric for the whole pineapple, so instead of pieces 9-56, you will only have one piece. I chose to appliqué each of the individual segments on the skin as I liked the three dimensional look that it gave to the fruit. Start the appliqué at the stem and the base first. Then appliqué the fruit and lastly appliqué the top leaves.

For templates, see next page.

Pineapple
(1 of 2)

Grapes

Grapes constitute the single largest fruit crop. It is a uniquely important food plant. It is estimated that there are as many as 10,000 varieties of grapes, yet only about a dozen or so of these are harvested for table grapes. The most common of these are the Thompson seedless. Most of our commercial grapes are grown in the central valley of California. Grapes are not only delicious to eat off the vine, they can be used in an assortment of savory dishes, made into jam and jelly, pressed for juice or wine or preserved for the rest of the year by drying into raisins. The tender leaves can be used as edible wrappings for meat and vegetables and even the seeds can be pressed and used for cooking oils.

Number of pattern pieces: 46

Fabrics needed

Fat quarters or scraps can be used. A mottled green batik was used for the leaves and a mottled purple batik was used for the grapes. The grapes can be red, green, purple or black.

Tip

The grapes were appliquéd on a 22" x 12" finished block. If you desire to use only one 12" block, appliqué only the bunch of grapes, the one leaf and the stem. Eliminate the leaves (43 and 45, the vines (42 and 44) and the stem (46). The grapes were all appliquéd individually, but with the right fabric with various shades of the grape color, the bunch could be cut out of one piece and the grapes can be shaped with quilting. Leave a section of leaf 1 open so stem 46 can be inserted. Leave the tip of leaf 45 free until after stem 46 is appliquéd in place.

For templates, see next page.

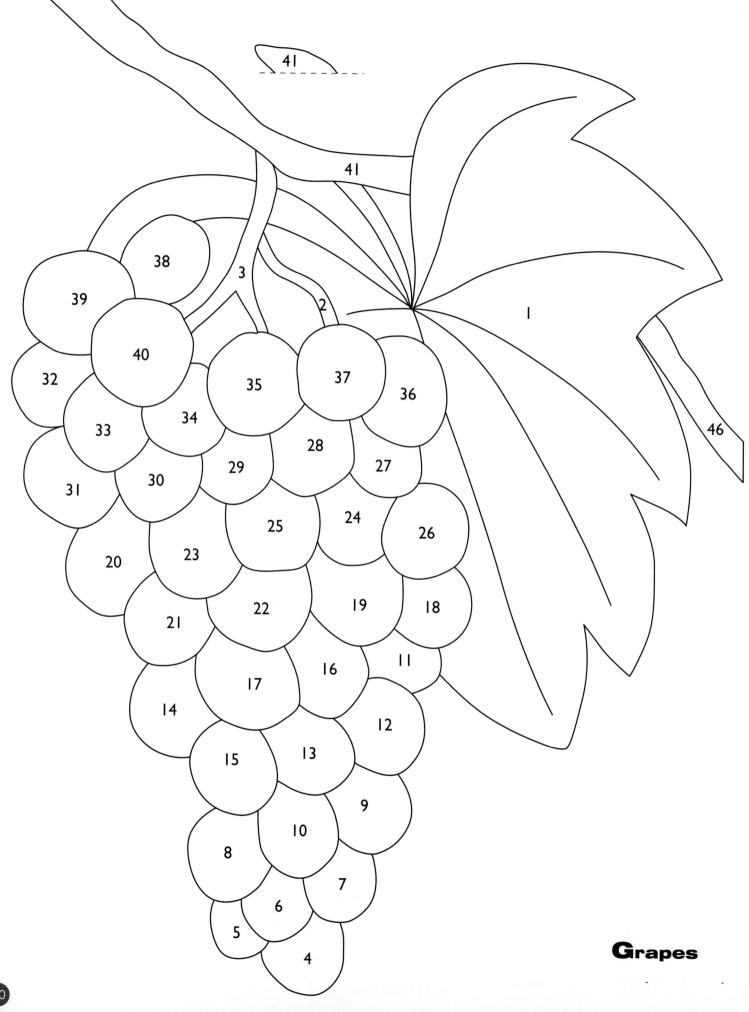

Grapes

80

Grapes

Cherries

*C*risp, dark sweet cherries are among our most precious culinary treasures. The best cherries need no preparation. Not all cherries are sweet, but sour cherries make fabulous pies, tarts, jams and cakes. Sour cherries are also used for liquors and brandy. The sour cherries are mostly grown in orchids in Michigan and New York and the sweet cherries come from Washington, Oregon and California. The growing season is very short—from late spring to early summer. The trees are very large and when in bloom with their pink and occasionally white blossoms, put on a memorable display.

Number of pattern pieces: 24

Fabrics needed

Fat quarters or scraps can be used. A mottled batik was used for the leaves and a mottled batik was used for the cherries.

Tip

The cherries were appliquéd on a 12" x 12" finished block. Leave a small area in branch 19 open to insert cherry stem 23, then appliqué the opening over the stems.

Pears closely resemble apples but they are not related. Although some pears are rounded, most pears are elongated. Pears are native to Europe and Asia, but were introduced to America in the 18th century. Most of the pears we eat come from Washington, Oregon and northern California, but some are also grown for market in the northeast. Pears have a very long growing season, extending from mid-summer through mid-winter. Most pears are eaten raw or added to salads of greens, nuts and cheese. Dessert pears are usually cooked into pies or tarts or poached in wine and served with ice cream.

Number of pattern pieces: 22

Fabrics needed

Fat quarters or scraps can be used. Two shades of green were used for the leaves. My pears were gold, however pears come in several shades and the choice is yours.

Tip

The pears were appliquéd on a 12" x 12" finished block. I shaded the core of the cut section of the pear with pale tan crayon and ironed to keep the color from washing out. The seeds may be appliquéd or embroidered with floss.

For templates, see next page.

Cherries

Pear

Plum

Plums are the most diverse group of the stone fruits and they come in more variations than most other fruits. They differ in season, size, shape, color and taste. Their color ranges from green through yellow to red, purple and blue; their flavor from sour to very sweet. The size and shape of plums is variable depending on the variety. Plums are native to Greece and Europe and were planted in Massachusetts in the seventeenth century. Most of our crop comes from California and the season lasts from late spring through fall. Plums can be eaten plain, used in jams, added to hardy stews and cooked into tarts.

Number of pattern pieces: 29

Fabrics needed

Fat quarters or scraps can be used. A mottled batik was used for the leaves and a mottled batik was used for the cherries.

Tip

The plums were appliquéd on a 12" x 12" finished block. The stamens were embroidered with 2 strands of black floss and yellow for French knots.

Kiwi

The kiwi is also known as the Chinese gooseberry. The kiwi was first grown commercially in New Zealand, but it originated in eastern Asia. They are now grown commercially in California. The fruit is slow to ripen and keeps well after being picked and so are easy to ship. The kiwi grows on strong vines which must be trained and pruned or they will form an unruly thicket. The wild kiwi vines have been grown on hillsides to control erosion. The fruit are oblong about two to three inches in length and an inch or two across. The skin is greenish brown and covered with fuzzy hair. The flesh is firm bright green with tiny edible black seeds. They are rich in vitamin C and can be eaten plain, added to salads, desserts and made into sherbets.

Number of pattern pieces: 23

Fabrics needed

Fat quarters or scraps can be used. A medium green fabric was used for the leaves, a brown fabric for the fruit and a lime green for the flesh.

Tip

The kiwi was appliquéd on a 12" x 12" finished block. The stems of the leaves 12, 13 and 14 were appliquéd with the leaf left loose until vine stem 15 was appliquéd in place. The black seeds on piece 23 were applied with a fine-point permanent marker. The stamens were embroidered with yellow floss.

For templates, see next page.

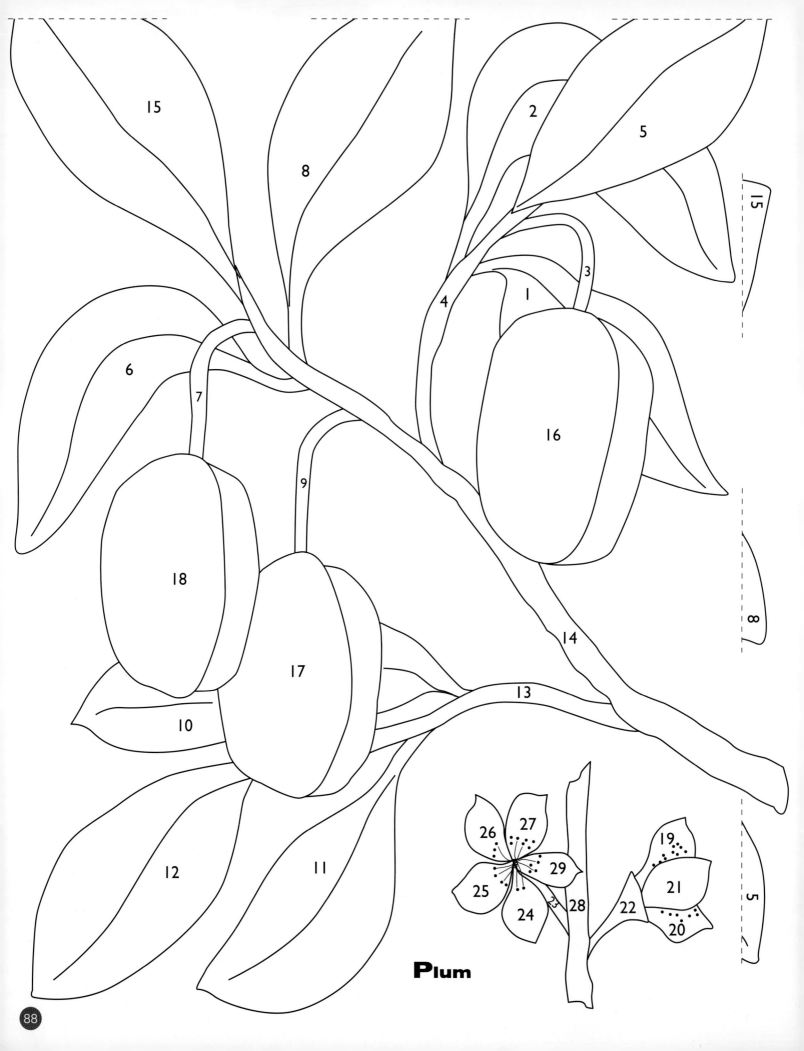

Plum

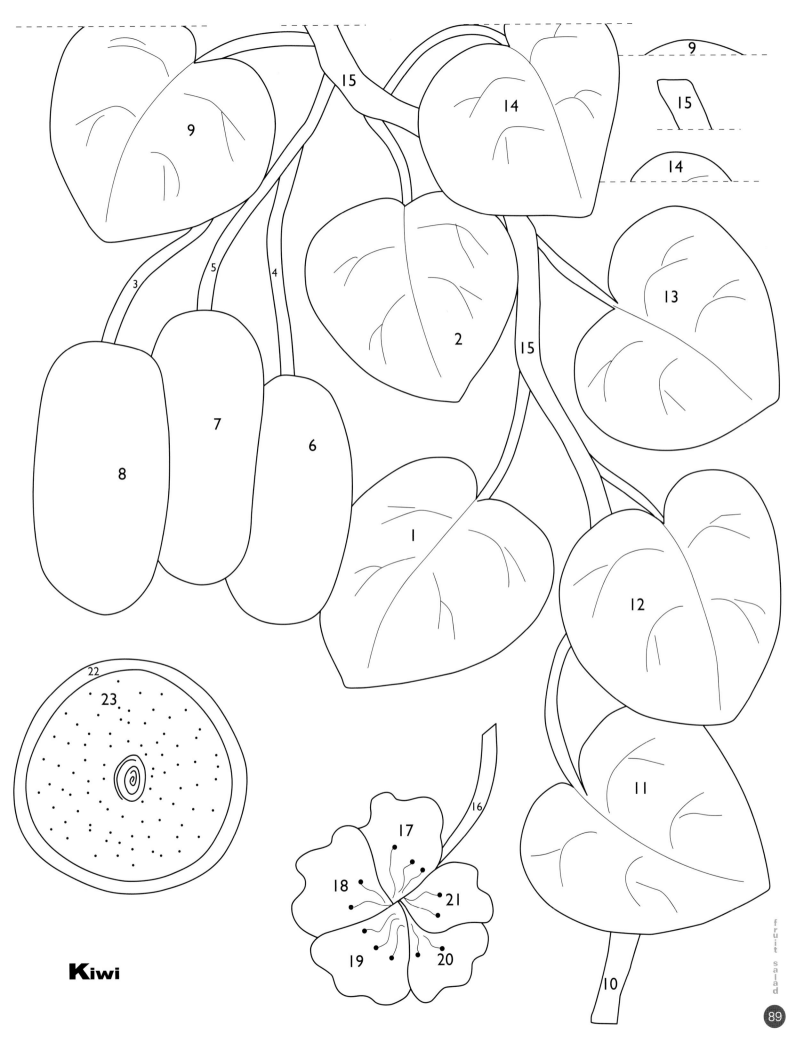

Kiwi

Melon

elons belong to a very large family. They all have tender, trailing vines that resemble cucumbers in their growing habits. They have large, broad leaves, and yellow flowers followed by the fruit that can be small to very large and round or oval. Melons were imported to the Western Hemisphere by Christopher Columbus on his second voyage, and their cultivation spread from the Caribbean as far north as New England. Melons are easy to grow as long as they have continual warmth. They start to ripen in June, but July and August are the best months. The melon is the most refreshing of our summer fruits.

Number of pattern pieces: 25

Fabrics needed

Fat quarters or scraps can be used. A mottled medium green batik fabric was used for the leaves and a deep green for the veins and vine. I chose the cantaloupe for my appliqué and used a dark orange for the melon, a brighter orange for the flesh and a light gold for the seeds.

Tip

The melon was appliquéd on a 25" x 12" finished block. If you want to make only one 12" block, use only the pieces 1-13. Leaves 10, 13, 16 and 22 were done in 2 parts. Appliqué the veins on the background first, then appliqué leaf section A and then section B over the vein. This will allow you to get very narrow veins. Leave a section of stem 17 open to insert vein 21.

For templates, see next page.

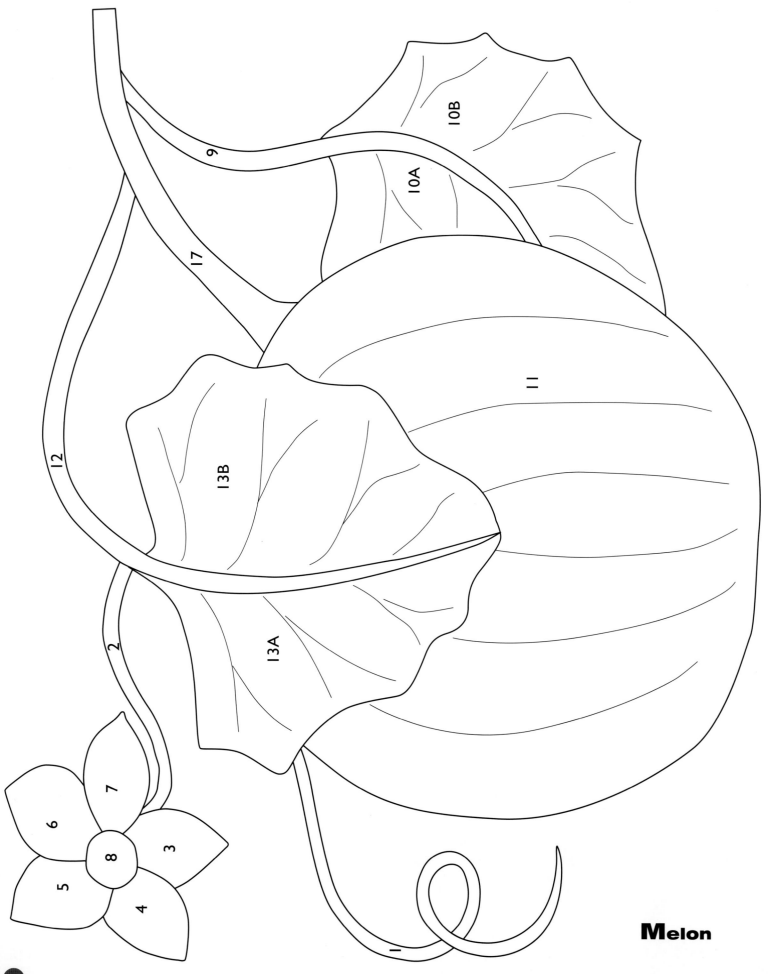

Melon

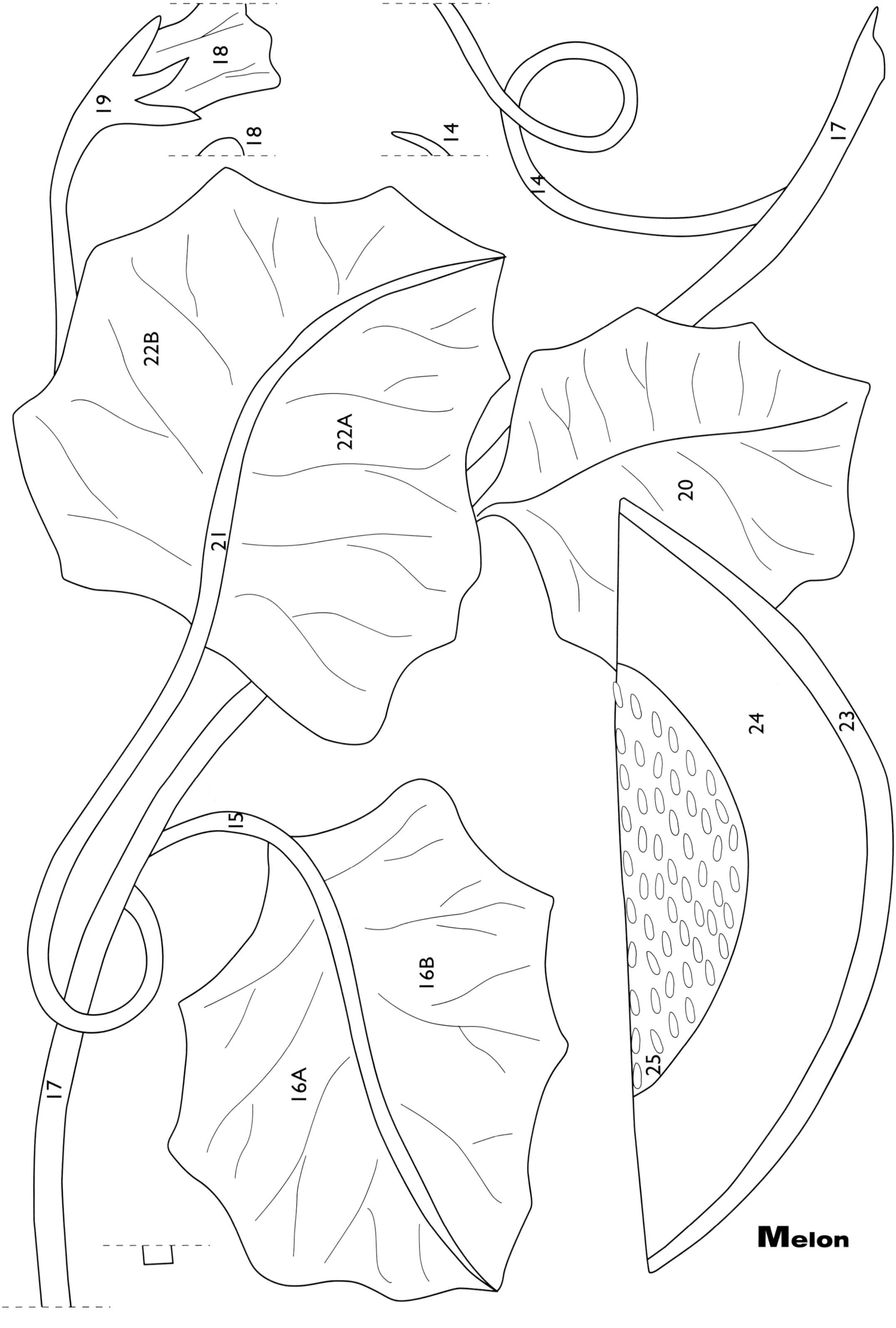

19

18

18

14

17

22B

22A

21

20

14

14

17

24

23

15

16B

16A

25

17

Melon

93

Border

5

4

1

3

2

15" x 4"

10" x 20"

4" x 21"

Pineapple

Use these templates for the Common Fruits wallhanging border. Arrange the pieces following the Assembly Diagram, above, and in full on page 69. The border uses 12 flowers, 3 single leaves, 9 double leaves and a freely-arranged bias trip vine.

About the Author

Bea Oglesby has been a quiltmaker, teacher and lecturer since 1990. Hand appliqué is her medium of choice and she finds a continual source of ideas in nature. Bea teaches and lectures in the Kansas City area and belongs to several quilt guilds. She volunteers weekly at the Johnson County Resource Library. Bea lives in Overland Park, Kansas with her husband Red. Since 2000, she has completed one quilt book every year. Her first Kansas City Star book, *Art Nouveau Quilts for the 21st Century* was published in 2006. *Alphabet Quilts: Letters for all Ages,* was published in 2007.

Download an additional free fruit pattern at www.TheKansasCityStore.com. Enter *"Still Life: Apples"* into the search field. Upon checkout, enter code **FS415BEA**.

One Piece at a Time by Kansas City Star Books – 1999

More Kansas City Star Quilts by Kansas City Star Books – 2000

Outside the Box: Hexagon Patterns from The Kansas City Star by Edie McGinnis – 2001

Prairie Flower: A Year on the Plains by Barbara Brackman – 2001

The Sister Blocks by Edie McGinnis – 2001

Kansas City Quiltmakers by Doug Worgul – 2001

O' Glory: Americana Quilts Blocks from The Kansas City Star by Edie McGinnis – 2001

Hearts and Flowers: Hand Appliqué from Start to Finish by Kathy Delaney – 2002

Roads and Curves Ahead: A Trip Through Time with Classic Kansas City Star Quilt Blocks by Edie McGinnis – 2002

Celebration of American Life: Appliqué Patterns Honoring a Nation and Its People by Barb Adams and Alma Allen – 2002

Women of Grace & Charm: A Quilting Tribute to the Women Who Served in World War II by Barb Adams and Alma Allen – 2003

A Heartland Album: More Techniques in Hand Appliqué by Kathy Delaney – 2003

Quilting a Poem: Designs Inspired by America's Poets by Frances Kite and Deb Rowden – 2003

Carolyn's Paper Pieced Garden: Patterns for Miniature and Full-Sized Quilts by Carolyn Cullinan McCormick – 2003

Friendships in Bloom: Round Robin Quilts by Marjorie Nelson and Rebecca Nelson-Zerfas – 2003

Baskets of Treasures: Designs Inspired by Life Along the River by Edie McGinnis – 2003

Heart & Home: Unique American Women and the Houses that Inspire by Kathy Schmitz – 2003

Women of Design: Quilts in the Newspaper by Barbara Brackman – 2004

The Basics: An Easy Guide to Beginning Quiltmaking by Kathy Delaney – 2004

Four Block Quilts: Echoes of History, Pieced Boldly & Appliquéd Freely by Terry Clothier Thompson – 2004

No Boundaries: Bringing Your Fabric Over the Edge by Edie McGinnis – 2004

Horn of Plenty for a New Century by Kathy Delaney – 2004

Quilting the Garden by Barb Adams and Alma Allen – 2004

Stars All Around Us: Quilts and Projects Inspired by a Beloved Symbol by Cherie Ralston – 2005

Quilters' Stories: Collecting History in the Heart of America by Deb Rowden – 2005

Libertyville: Where Liberty Dwells, There is My Country by Terry Clothier Thompson – 2005

Sparkling Jewels, Pearls of Wisdom by Edie McGinnis – 2005

Grapefruit Juice and Sugar: Bold Quilts Inspired by Grandmother's Legacy by Jenifer Dick – 2005

Home Sweet Home by Barb Adams and Alma Allen – 2005

Patterns of History: The Challenge Winners by Kathy Delaney – 2005

My Quilt Stories by Debra Rowden – 2005

Quilts in Red and Green and the Women Who Made Them by Nancy Hornback and Terry Clothier Thompson – 2006

Hard Times, Splendid Quilts: A 1930s Celebration, Paper Piecing from The Kansas City Star by Carolyn Cullinan McCormick – 2006

Art Nouveau Quilts for the 21st Century by Bea Oglesby – 2006

Designer Quilts: Great Projects from Moda's Best Fabric Artists – 2006

Birds of a Feather by Barb Adams and Alma Allen – 2006

Feedsacks! Beautiful Quilts from Humble Beginnings by Edie McGinnis – 2006

Kansas Spirit: Historical Quilt Blocks and the Saga of the Sunflower State by Jeanne Poore – 2006

Bold Improvisation: Searching for African-American Quilts – The Heffley Collection by Scott Heffley – 2007

The Soulful Art of African-American Quilts: Nineteen Bold, Improvisational Projects by Sonie Ruffin – 2007

Alphabet Quilts: Letters for All Ages by Bea Oglesby – 2007

Beyond the Basics: A Potpourri of Quiltmaking Techniques by Kathy Delaney – 2007

Golden's Journal: 20 Sampler Blocks Honoring Prairie Farm Life by Christina DeArmond, Eula Lang and Kaye Spitzli – 2007

Borderland in Butternut and Blue: A Sampler Quilt to Recall the Civil War Along the Kansas/Missouri Border by Barbara Brackman – 2007

Come to the Fair: Quilts that Celebrate State Fair Traditions by Edie McGinnis – 2007

Cotton and Wool: Miss Jump's Farewell by Linda Brannock – 2007

You're Invited! Quilts and Homes to Inspire by Barb Adams and Alma Allen, Blackbird Designs – 2007

Portable Patchwork: Who Says You Can't Take it With You? by Donna Thomas – 2008

Quilts for Rosie: Paper Piecing Patterns from the '40s by Carolyn Cullinan McCormick – 2008

Fruit Salad: Appliqué Designs for Delicious Quilts by Bea Oglesby – 2008

Red, Green and Beyond: Yesterday's Appliqué for Today's Quilters by Nancy Hornback and Terry Clothier Thompson – 2008

Queen Bees Mysteries:

Murders on Elderberry Road by Sally Goldenbaum – 2003

A Murder of Taste by Sally Goldenbaum – 2004

Murder on a Starry Night by Sally Goldenbaum – 2005

Queen Bees Murder Mystery 4 by Marnette Falley – 2008

Project Books:

Fan Quilt Memories by Jeanne Poore – 2000

Santa's Parade of Nursery Rhymes by Jeanne Poore – 2001

As the Crow Flies by Edie McGinnis – 2007

Sweet Inspirations by Pam Manning – 2007

Quilts Through the Camera's Eye by Terry Clothier Thompson – 2007

Louisa May Alcott: Quilts of Her Life, Her Work, Her Heart by Terry Clothier Thompson – 2008

The Lincoln Museum Quilt: A Reproduction for Abe's Frontier Cabin by Barbara Brackman and Deb Rowden – 2008